Handbells in the Liturgical Service

MT
711
.F64
1984

Handbells in the Liturgical Service

John Folkening

**Church Music Pamphlet Series
Carl Schalk, Editor**

60140

CONCORDIA COLLEGE LIBRARY
BRONXVILLE, N. Y. 10708

Copyright © 1984 Concordia Publishing House
3558 S. Jefferson Avenue, St. Louis, MO 63118
Manufactured in the United States of America

All rights reserved. No part of this publication may be reproduced, stored in a retrieval system, or transmitted, in any form or by any means, electronic, mechanical, photocopying, recording, or otherwise, without the prior written permission of Concordia Publishing House.

1 2 3 4 5 6 7 8 9 10   WP   93 92 91 90 89 88 87 86 85 84

Contents

Bells in the Worship of the Church	7
Handbells in Liturgical Worship	11
Handbells and Ringing Techniques	13
Notational and Harmonic Considerations	15
Using Handbells in the Liturgy	17
Giving Pitches	17
Accompanying Psalm Chants	20
Enriching the Great Songs of the Liturgy	25
Processions	28
Accompanying Hymns	31
Appendix A: Using Handbells in Divine Service II, *Lutheran Worship (LW)*	38
Appendix B: Using Handbells in the Service of Holy Communion, *Lutheran Book of Worship (LBW)*	39
Appendix C: Using Handbells in the Service of Morning Prayer	40
Appendix D: Using Handbells in the Service of Evening Prayer	41
Appendix E: Suggestions for Further Reading	42
Appendix F: Handbell Organization and Principal Manufacturers of Handbells	43
Notes	44
Acknowledgments	45

Bells in the Worship of the Church

The use of handbells for a variety of religious purposes was widespread throughout the ancient world and is readily documented. The oldest extant handbells come from China and are dated about 1600 B.C. Handbells are found in Egypt as early as the 8th century B.C., in India from the 5th or 6th centuries B.C., in Japan from the 6th century A.D., as well as in Africa, where handbells are indigenous to religious rites in many parts of that continent.[1]

Bells of many varieties have long been associated with Christian worship. Missionaries on their way from Africa to western Europe brought handbells with them. Likewise the early Celts were also instrumental in the introduction of bells to western and central Europe, although the early, larger bells were shaped like a rectangular box and must

Figures playing various instruments, among them bells. (Date unknown)

have had a rather dull tone. The familiar contour of the larger church bell was introduced in the Gothic period, and with it the typical sound of the church bell as we know it today.

In the Middle Ages, bells played an important part in helping to regulate the daily life of the people. In 13th-century France, for example, bells were rung at six in the morning (the *Ave Maria* bells), at noon, and in the evening for vespers. Somewhat later, these bells rung at morning, midday, and evening were called the *Angelus* bells.

Many old customs are associated with the ringing of church bells. These include the "curfew bell," originally the signal to cover the fire, extinguish all lights, and retire for the night; the "harvest bell" and the "seeding bell," which announced the hours for the beginning and ending of gleaning; the "marker bell," which was the signal for selling to begin in the town; and the "passing bell," rung for the dying, and later rung after death.

Martin Luther's writings reflect some of these traditional uses for bells as, for example, when he noted their use on August 18, 1532, upon the death of Elector John Frederick of Saxony and remarked that "the ringing of bells sounds different than usual when one knows that the deceased is somebody one loves."[2] And in his "Instructions for the Visitors of Parish Pastors in Electoral Saxony" (1528), Luther had the following to say about the use of bells:

> it would not be amiss if in summertime the preacher explained to the people when storms threatened and the bells were rung, that the reason for the custom was not that the sound of the bells or the consecration of the bells drove away the storm or the frost, as had been taught and believed hitherto, but that thereby each one should be reminded to pray to God for his protection of the fruits of the earth. . . .
>
> If now the ringing is done away with the people will probably be less often reminded that God determines the weather, and will that much less call on God.[3]

Luther also remarked that "ringing the *Pacem* is in many places meant to let the people know the time of morning, or of evening when it is time to leave the fields for home."[4]

But smaller bells were also in evidence in connection with the music and worship of the church. As early as the 6th century, Martin of Tours reports that small cup-shaped bells (*cymbala*) were suspended above the performer and used as instruments in the liturgical worship of the church. These early forerunners of the modern handbell were struck with chisel-like hammers and, together with a variety of other instruments, gradually found their way into the church's worship. In a logical extension of their use, handles were added to the bells, enabling them to be carried in procession. Such processional bells were apparently used to maintain pitch and momentum in the singing of the psalms and to signal the beginning of new phrases or breathing points. Thus, especially in monastic services, the punctuating of psalms with bell notes served as a pace-setting device, while also reinforcing needed pitches. Historically, it was the percussive quality of the bells that characterized their use more than their melodic characteristics.

The earliest manuscripts reflecting the use of handbells in western Europe date from about the 13th century, about the same time that small bells began to be tuned in a diatonic series. Handbells may well have been used in music of the late medieval and early Renaissance periods in connection with both singers and instrumentalists, although the musical notation does not specifically call for them.

The Puritan movement in 17th-century England suppressed the use of bells, but a new use was found for them as rehearsal instruments for the new change-ringing of church bells, which was coming into fashion. Complex "changes," or systems of ringing large numbers of church tower bells in repeated patterns, were practiced daily in many villages throughout England. The resulting disturbance to the surrounding villagers, as well as the cold and damp conditions of the churches, made practicing with smaller handbells a highly desirable alternative.

Over a period of time the smaller handbells came to be used not only as practice instruments but as performance instruments as well. By the mid-19th century virtually every English village had its own handbell team.

About the middle of the 19th century groups of handbell ringers, many of them immigrant families, began to tour the eastern United States, especially in the Chautauqua programs and vaudeville circuits. P.T. Barnum included a group of so-called Swiss bell ringers in his traveling shows, exposing many Americans to handbell ringing. In more recent years there has been a growing interest in the art of handbell ringing throughout the United States, particularly through the efforts of The American Guild of English Handbell Ringers. Handbells produced by a variety of manufacturers in the United States, England, and Holland are enjoying widespread popularity, and their use in corporate worship is increasingly widespread.

Bell chimes from the Portail Royal of the Cathedral of Chartres, 12th century

Figure playing bells. (Date unknown)

Handbells in Liturgical Worship

As with all the music of worship — whether that of congregation, choir, organ, soloist, or other instruments — *handbells find their chief function in leading and participating in the liturgical worship of the people.* Whether bells function in connection with the singing of the people, the choir, the presiding or assisting ministers, the organ, or even alone, in the best Lutheran tradition *they always function liturgically.* As the church musician considers integrating handbells into the total music program of the parish, it is essential that this goal be kept clearly in mind.

While the use of handbells in a concert setting may well require several octaves of bells and many highly trained ringers, the liturgical use of bells may necessitate the use of only a few bells and a few ringers. While handbells used in this way may not produce the spectacular show and flair desirable for a concert, they are nonetheless most effective liturgically when they lead the congregation to an ever-increasing participation in the liturgy. Simplicity and restraint in the use of bells in such circumstances becomes an asset rather then a liability.

Too often handbell music intended for performance (regardless of a "religious" title) is simply injected into the liturgy. When this occurs, the liturgy effectively comes to a halt and the congregation becomes an audience rather than a participating partner in the liturgy. Church musicians will have to come to see that the simple giving of a pitch with a handbell or the use of handbells in introducing and accompanying a psalm sung by the congregation is more central to a liturgical use of handbells than is a more complicated performance of a handbell "anthem."

As with any music in worship, the use of handbells in the liturgical service should be based on their function in worship, rather than on their entertainment value or the complexity of their performance. The church musician may well discover that in order to use handbells properly and effectively within the liturgical worship, simple selections or settings may have to be composed to fill the needs of a particular service. Such simple compositions or adaptations of existing material are often within the musical capabilities of many parish musicians.

A French miniature initial in a Psalter from the first half of the 13th century

From a 14th-century manuscript showing organ, chimes, psaltery, and a figure holding two bells in one hand

Handbells and Ringing Techniques

The illustration in figure 1 depicts a handbell with its basic parts identified. The player grips the leather or plastic *handle* with fingers wrapped all the way around the strap. Fingers should not be inserted through the loop of the handle, although to the novice this may seem to be the safest grip. The index finger and thumb should rest solidly against the *collar,* the round piece located just below the *bell casting*. While holding the bell at shoulder height, the wrist is tilted backward toward the player's body so that the *clapper* rests near the side of the bell. To ring the bell, a quick snap of the wrist coupled with a smooth forearm motion, similar to cracking a whip, sends the clapper swinging to the opposite side of the bell, where it strikes the bell casting and produces the tone.

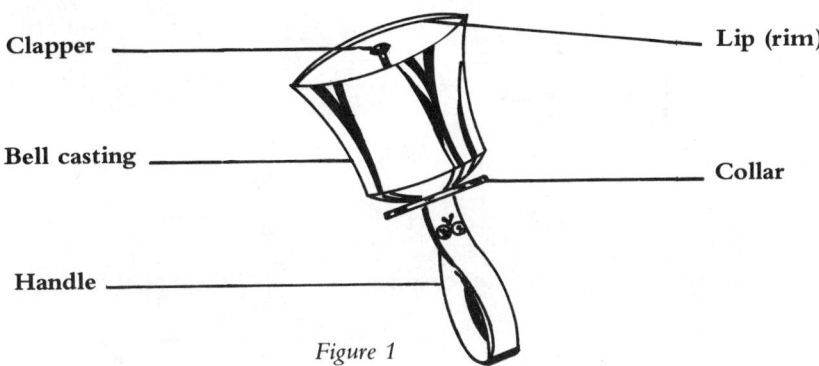

Figure 1

Although there are many sophisticated techniques in handbell ringing to achieve various tonal effects, the essentials for producing good handbell tone are simple. Keep the motion of the clapper always in line with the motion of the wrist and arm, avoid unnecessary arm swinging, and keep the wrist action crisp.

It is important to realize where the bell tone originates and how to maximize the sound. Handbell tone does not come out of the mouth of the bell as it does in a trumpet or megaphone. Rather, the sound waves proceed outward from the rim of the bell, perpendicular to the handle. Thus aiming the bell at the intended audience actually sends the sound down to the floor, up to the ceiling, and to the side walls. The bells, having been rung, should always be returned to the upright position so that the maximum sound is dispersed to the audience.

The tone of the bell is "damped" by touching the bell to the shoulder of the ringer. A gloved hand may also be used to stop the tone if the ringer is assigned only one bell. Gloves are always worn when ringing bells to avoid marring them with smudges or fingerprints which, if left untreated, could eventually etch permanent marks into the surface of the bells.

From a Würzburg-Ebrach Psalter. The initial "B" showing many instruments, among them bells.

Notational and Harmonic Considerations

Before considering the use of handbells in the liturgy, it is important to recognize certain notational and harmonic features of handbells. The chart in figure 2 indicates the standard groupings of handbell sets, as well as their designated pitch names. All handbell parts sound one octave higher than written. Thus C5, or middle C on the piano, will sound an octave above middle C when played on a handbell.

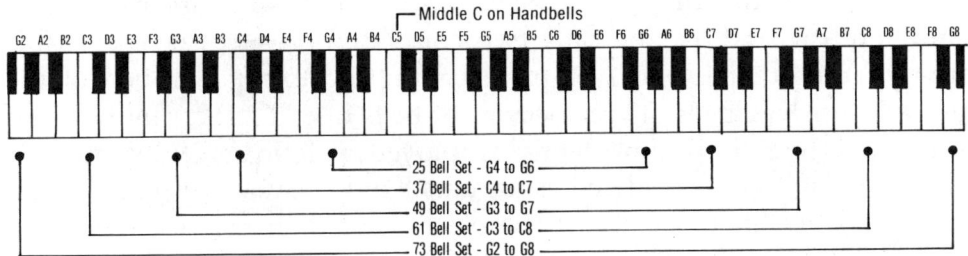

Figure 2

The tone that is produced by a handbell is characterized by a full-sounding *fundamental* or "strike tone," as well as by a rich variety of *overtones*. Depending on how they are constructed, different overtones may be accented. The "Flemish school" of bell making accents the minor third above the fundamental pitch as a principal overtone. As a result, harmonies containing thirds and sixths tend to sound dissonant on such bells. The "English school" of bell making avoids the minor third as a principal overtone and accents instead the fifth above the fundamental as the chief overtone. Thus harmonies containing thirds and sixths sound quite pleasant on such bells.

The earliest manuscripts of handbell music reflect the tonal and harmonic structure of polyphony that regards fourths and fifths as primary consonant intervals. Octaves and seconds also fall into this category. Dissonant intervals included major and minor sixths, and the lack of thirds in medieval music suggests that they were not held in high regard as principal consonant intervals. Seconds, fourths, fifths, and octaves dominated as consonant sounds that carried well in the setting of medieval worship.

While the use of thirds is not necessarily excluded in present-day handbell music, most of the examples in this pamphlet will attempt to echo the older intervalic preferences. The "open" sound of fourths and fifths is both ancient and modern in its tonal structure and works well in contemporary uses of handbells in liturgical music.

Although sets of handbells ranging from two to six octaves are available for purchase from handbell manufacturers, it is important to keep in mind the primary function of handbells in the liturgical service. If liturgical participation within the framework of worship is the chief function of handbells, then the five- and six-octave sets could represent an excessive number of bells that may not be played enough to warrant their purchase. On the other hand, having only two complete octaves of bells available greatly limits the potential of participation and excludes much of the literature for handbells. Three octaves of bells offer a rather full range of tones, which may be consistently employed in liturgical worship, and therefore might be considered as an initial and adequate set under most circumstances. Should a fourth octave be added, it could certainly be utilized should the number of ringers and the expanded repertoire call for it.

Using Handbells in the Liturgy

The following sections describe several basic ways in which handbells may function in a unique and effective way in the liturgical service. These sections, together with the musical examples given in each section, offer suggestions for integrating the use of handbells carefully and sensitively into the liturgical service. They will need to be carefully evaluated and adapted to the particular circumstances of specific parishes and their resources. The services that are addressed in this chapter are Holy Communion (Hillert setting) and Morning and Evening Prayer, services common to both *Lutheran Book of Worship* and *Lutheran Worship*.

Giving Pitches

One of the most practical uses of handbells in the liturgical service may be found in the very necessary task of giving pitches, either to assisting or presiding ministers at various points within the service or occasionally to the choir or cantor. The suggestions in this section deal particularly with giving pitches to the assisting and presiding ministers.

Giving pitches is necessary in two circumstances: (1) the first time a pitch is needed by one leading in worship, usually at the beginning of a particular order; and (2) in the course of the liturgy when, after sections of spoken liturgy the basic tonality of the musical setting may have been forgotten, it may be helpful to reestablish the pitch.

Two basic types of pitch patterns may be used in services where the liturgy is sung: *single pitches* and *multiple pitch* patterns. Single pitches are given when the initial note of the chant is sustained or is itself the tonic pitch of the chant. The examples below are the only instances where single pitches need be given in Holy Communion and Evening Prayer. (It may not even be necessary under most circumstances to give the pitch to the presiding minister at the time of the Salutation prior to the Prayer of the Day since this pitch can easily be obtained from the last note of the Hymn of Praise.)

Multiple pitch patterns may be given when the chanted line does not begin on a sustained pitch or when the tonic is approached by other pitches. The following examples are the only instances in Holy Communion and Morning Prayer where such multiple pitch patterns need be given. (There are no such instances in Evening Prayer.)

It is also possible that a musically trained minister or cantor could be given only the third pitch in the examples above and use it as the tonic to find the opening pitch of the three-note pattern.

Whatever the case, it is important that the person chanting have an opportunity to practice with the handbells so that he or she becomes accustomed to their unique blend of fundamental pitch and overtones. The sound of pitches given by handbells is different from the timbre of the organ, making rehearsal of pitch-giving necessary, at least until the practice becomes familiar and comfortable.

Three general suggestions for giving pitches with handbells may be helpful.

1. *Use handbells for giving pitches sparingly and discreetly.* Constantly giving pitches at every possible opportunity should be avoided. It can easily become an obtrusive element, as has the common practice of giving pitches at the organ.

2. *Allow the sound of the bells to die out before beginning the sung intonation.* This not only allows the pitch to become more firmly established in the mind of the person intoning, it also gives the liturgy a more deliberate pace. Especially when bells are used to give the pitch at the beginning of Morning or Evening Prayer or at the time of the Kyrie petitions at the beginning of Holy Communion, the sound of the bells not only serves to give a necessary pitch, it also signals to the congregation the beginning of the liturgy. Allowing the sound of the bell to die away before beginning the intonation gives the congregation adequate time to attune their hearts and minds to what is to follow.

3. *As a parish becomes increasingly familiar with a particular musical setting of the liturgy, many worship leaders will find it possible to "remember" the basic tonal centers — even after longer stretches of spoken liturgy — and may not need as frequent reminders of the pitch.* This will depend, of course, on the general musical ability and musical sensitivity of the various worship leaders.

The goal of using handbells in giving pitches in the course of the liturgy is to give pitches only when absolutely necessary. Many portions of the service flow directly from one to another and the repetition of pitches each time may not be necessary. Cantors, assisting and presiding ministers, and other worship leaders will have to decide in their particular situation just when such pitches are necessary.

Accompanying Psalm Chants

The singing of the psalms, whether by congregation, choir, solo voice, or some combination of these, offers perhaps the greatest potential for the creative use of handbells. Psalm tones, whether Gregorian or contemporary, whether found in *Lutheran Book of Worship* or *Lutheran Worship*, are, by their very nature, well-suited for accompaniment, rhythmic punctuation, and the use of ostinato figures by handbells.

Besides giving the pitch or intonation for the psalm tone, handbells may be played in clusters at the midpoint and conclusion of psalm verses to punctuate rhythmically the tone. A great advantage of such punctuation is that only a few bells are required for simple chords or clusters, although more bells may be used, doubling at various octaves as the circumstances may dictate, if they are available. Thus many options are open to the creative church musician.

The sensitive church musician will want to let the season of the church year, the nature of a particular festival, and the character of the psalm itself dictate the musical resources to be used. Obviously, a handbell accompaniment for the psalm appointed for Ash Wednesday will differ greatly from the psalm appointed for Easter Day. Handbells offer a full spectrum of tonal effects, ranging from the lean, open sounds of seconds, fourths, and fifths to the richness of more complex clusters doubled or tripled at the octave.

The following examples demonstrate various ways that handbells can be used to accompany three commonly employed formulary systems of psalm tones: the Gregorian psalm tones, those in *Lutheran Book of Worship,* and those in *Lutheran Worship.* A sufficient number of tones in each of these formulary systems is given so that the church musician can see this idea at work and apply it to other tones as needed. Some church musicians may wish to compose their own tones, following the patterns given here and using the resources at his or her disposal. In all cases, once the handbells have been struck, they are permitted to ring without being damped by the ringer. Such ringing serves as a helpful bridge between sections of the tone, and any resulting dissonances are readily accepted by the ear.

The first example, which gives Psalm 117 in its entirety, uses simple *clusters of chords* to give the pitch and punctuate the midpoint and conclusion of each verse. Following the punctuation at the conclusion of the first psalm verse, the choir (or congregation or soloist) proceeds immediately to the second verse.

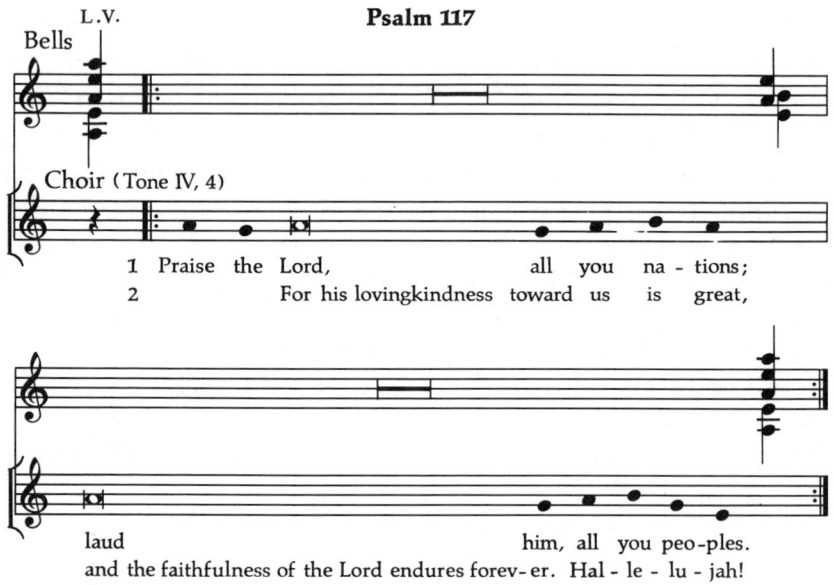

The second example uses an *ostinato figure* based on the same bell notes that are used in the first example. Once the ostinato pattern begins, there should be no attempt to synchronize the bell pattern with the singing of the choir or congregation. The choir and bells proceed simultaneously, but nonsynchronously.

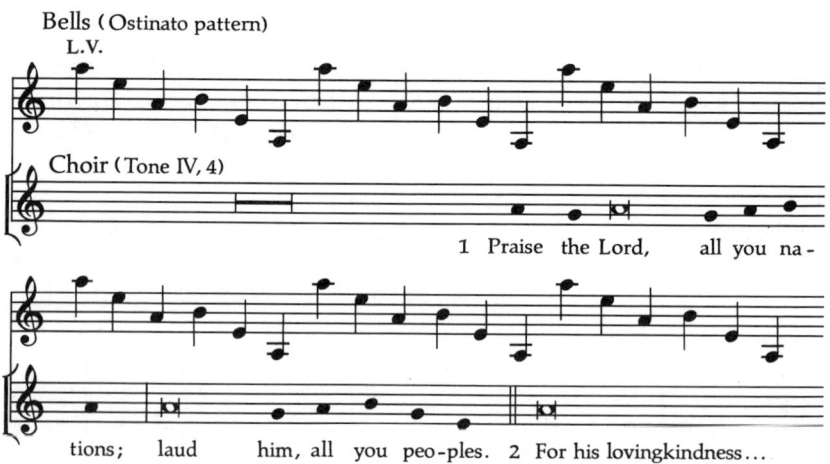

Still a third way of adapting this idea is to allow the ringers to ring their various bells in a *random pattern*, each ringer ringing his or her bell in a completely spontaneous or aleatory fashion. Such random ringing gives a more spontaneous and festive character to the entire singing of the psalm.

The following charts indicate specific tone clusters that may be used with some of the more familiar tones from the Gregorian repertoire, as well as tones from *Lutheran Book of Worship* and *Lutheran Worship*. These clusters may be doubled or tripled at various octaves depending on the number of bells available and the number of singers who are being accompanied. Some church musicians may wish to write their own clusters.

Gregorian Psalm Tones

Enriching the Great Songs of the Liturgy

Certain of the great liturgical songs offer a particular opportunity when the sound of bells can add appreciably to the festive nature of the celebration. Such great songs as the Hymn of Praise ("Glory to God in the highest" and "This is the feast of victory for our God") or the canticles from Morning and Evening Prayer come to mind. Settings of these and other songs which sensitively use bells to enhance the mood of the particular liturgical song can be especially effective on occasion.

Such a climactic point in the liturgy as at the singing of the "Holy, Holy, Holy" in the Holy Communion offers a particularly excellent opportunity to enrich the solemnity and festive joy of this great liturgical song with the addition of bells. The following setting is but one example of the way in which such an enrichment might take place.

In a similar fashion, the great song of thanksgiving following the distribution of Holy Communion, "Thank the Lord and sing his praise,"

would be another example of one of the great songs of the liturgy that could well include the festive ringing of bells. The following setting is merely one way in which this might be accomplished.

Processions

The liturgy incorporates several kinds of processions among the various orders of service. There is the entrance processional which is often a congregational hymn but may also be a psalm. There is the procession at the time of the Gospel, often utilized on great festivals of the church year and at other appropriate times. There is the procession at the time of the bringing forward of the gifts. In Evening Prayer there is a procession in connection with the Service of Light. Each has its particular character and particular liturgical requirements as far as the music that accompanies each procession is concerned.

The striking of a single handbell, or two handbells at the interval of a fourth or fifth, simultaneously or in succession, can be an effective means of establishing and maintaining momentum in a procession of choir or clergy. The regularly timed striking of bells gives a sense of expectation and reverence in its simplicity.

When the choir processes, either at the beginning or end of the service, handbells might be employed on occasion to mark their entrance or exit and to pace their step. Particularly on great festivals of the church year, a processional hymn chanted by the choir and accompanied only by bells can be especially effective. An offertory procession could also utilize handbells as a special accompaniment to the bringing forward of bread, wine, and other offerings, perhaps using bells in the same key as the proper Offertory sung by the choir. Handbells are especially appropriate in the procession in connection with the Service of Light in Evening Prayer, in which case the organ should certainly not be employed. In the absence of a fanfare at the time of the Gospel procession, handbells could be used to mark the procession of the Gospel to and from the center of the nave. The percussive quality of handbells makes their participation in processions both practical and effective.

Two examples are given here. The first, "Of the Father's Love Begotten," is one of the greatest of Christmas hymns. Its appointment as the Hymn of the Day for Christmas makes it available not only for choir but for congregation as well. Sung each Christmas in stark simplicity by choir and congregation accompanied only by handbells, this hymn could easily become a welcome procession tradition in many parishes. Depending on the size of the congregation, it may be necessary to double the pitches of the bells at various octaves.

have _____ been, And that fu-ture years shall see
Ev - er - more and ev - er - more. _____

The second example of a processional hymn, "Creator Spirit, Heavenly Dove," is one of the great Pentecost hymns and, while usually sung at all ordinations, may also be used as a general hymn of invocation of the Holy Spirit. This simple setting could be sung by the choir accompanied only by bells, alternating with the congregation singing the simpler form of the melody found in both *Lutheran Book of Worship* and *Lutheran Worship*. It could also be sung entirely by the choir, all stanzas being sung to the following chant form.

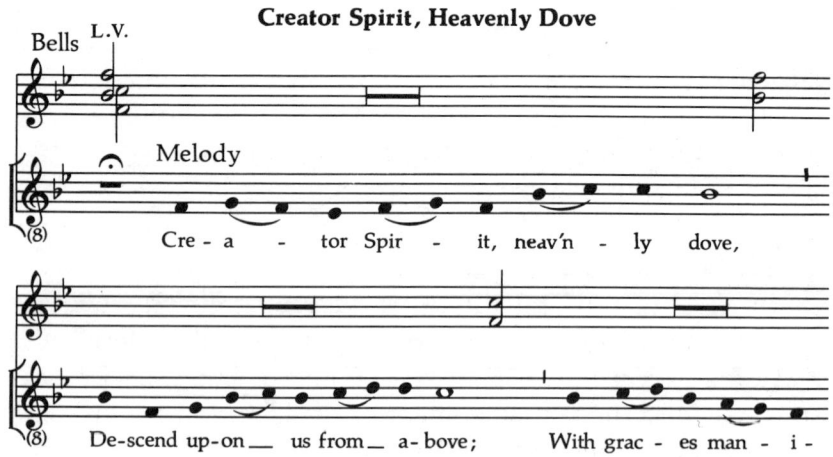

Creator Spirit, Heavenly Dove

Bells L.V.

Melody

Cre - a - tor Spir - it, heav'n - ly dove,
De-scend up-on __ us from __ a- bove; With grac - es man - i-

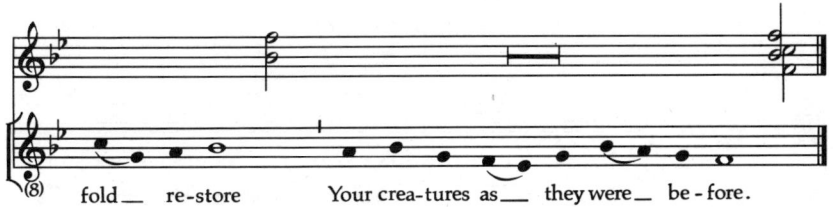

Accompanying Hymns

Generally, handbells are least effective with congregational singing when they are used simply to play the four-part accompaniment from the hymnal. Handbell tone is usually too light and delicate to support such singing by the entire congregation. But the use of handbells in connection with congregational singing of hymns can effectively employ a variety of techniques that capitalize on the rhythmic or harmonic characteristics of particular hymn tunes.

The following paragraphs discuss four basic ways of using handbells in connection with congregational singing: punctuation of cadences with chord clusters; use of block chords coinciding with the larger pulse of the hymn; use of ostinato chord patterns; and random ringing of many bells in the tonality of the hymn.

Punctuation of Cadences with Chord Clusters

A particularly effective method of handbell accompaniment to hymns is to punctuate the endings of phrases or cadences with clusters of tone. The two examples following illustrate such punctuation in much the same manner described earlier in connection with psalm singing. Such settings often sound best when accompanying smaller groups of voices or segments of the congregation (such as all the treble voices in the hymn alternation). As with the psalm tone accompaniments, the handbell resources may range from the very sparse sound of only a few bells to the richer texture of larger numbers of bells. The particular service, season of the church year, and the textual content of the hymn or hymn stanza will help to further determine the best handling of the bells.

Gelobt sei Gott

Picardy

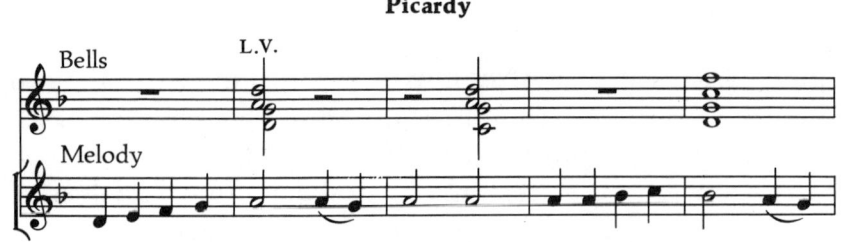

Use of Block Chords

A second effective method of hymn accompaniment employs block chords played to coincide with the larger pulse of the hymn tune. One or two such chords per measure not only offer the possibility for great harmonic interest and vitality but also provide momentum and drive to the pulse of the hymn itself.

The following examples illustrate this technique. If used in conjunction with the organ, the bell chords must obviously be compatible with the organ accompaniment of a given stanza. If used alone, without the organ, as in the following two examples, such harmonic restrictions are not necessary. The use of bells and unison choir, for example, as an alternate stanza in a hymn alternation, is an effective way of using this technique. The chords may be expanded to include a larger number of bells, depending on the resources available and the particular circumstances.

In Babilone

Earth and All Stars

35

Use of Ostinato Chord Pattern

The use of ostinato-like chord patterns is a third method of hymn accompaniment. The bells of each chord are rung and permitted to fade slowly without being damped. The resulting dissonances and "chance" harmonies can provide a unique and beautiful background for the hymn tune. In such cases, the ostinato pattern may, if desired, be played through once completely as an intonation to the stanza. The following setting of *St. Columba* illustrates this technique.

St. Columba

Random Ringing Within the Tonality of a Hymn

Finally, on festive occasions, it may be desirable to enhance the joyful nature of a hymn, particularly on a final or doxological stanza, by ringing at random many bells that are contained within the tonality of the hymn. This type of "peal," not unlike that created by the Zimbelstern of the pipe organ, creates an aura of sound around the hymn tune that sparkles and cascades over and over. This device is most effective when used together with the organ accompaniment to the hymn and the full congregation.

The following example of *Duke Street* illustrates this technique. Obviously, such a device could easily become tedious and trite if used too frequently. But its careful and judicious use on special occasions — particularly on the great festivals of the church — can add a new degree of brilliance and life to stanzas of great joy, praise, and doxology.

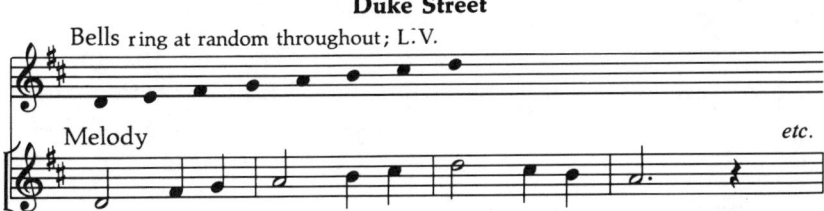

Appendix A
Using Handbells in Divine Service II, *Lutheran Worship (LW)*

Portion of Service	Handbell Use
Hymn of Invocation	
Confession and Absolution	
Introit, Psalm, or Entrance Hymn	Psalm Tone Accompaniment
Kyrie	Intonation pitches
Hymn of Praise	
Collect of the Day	
Old Testament Reading	
Gradual or Psalm	Psalm Tone Accompaniment
Epistle	
Verse	
Gospel	
Hymn of the Day	
Sermon	
Creed	
Prayers	
Offering	
Offertory	Played during Procession
Preface	Intonation pitches
Sanctus	Accompaniment
Lord's Prayer	
Words of Institution	
Peace	
Agnus Dei	
Communion	
Post-Communion Canticle	Accompaniment
Prayer	
Benediction	Pitch given

Appendix B
Using Handbells in the Service of Holy Communion,
Lutheran Book of Worship (LBW)

Portion of Service	Handbell Use
Brief Order for Confession	
Entrance Hymn	
Kyrie	Intonation pitches
Hymn of Praise	
Prayer of the Day	
First Lesson	
Psalm	Psalm Tone Accompaniment
Second Lesson	
Verse	
Gospel	Intonation pitches
Sermon	
Hymn of the Day	
Creed	
Prayers	
Peace	
Offering	
Offertory	Played during Procession
Great Thanksgiving	Intonation pitches
Sanctus	Accompaniment
Words of Institution	
Lord's Prayer	Single pitch (if chanted)
Communion	
Post-Communion Canticle	Accompaniment
Prayer	
Benediction	Pitch given

Appendix C
Using Handbells in the Service of Morning Prayer

Portion of Service	**Handbell Use**
Opening Versicles	Pitch given
Psalmody	Pitch given
Second Psalm (opt. *LW*)	Psalm Tone Accompaniment
Psalm Prayer (*LBW*)	
Hymn	
Reading(s)	
Gospel Canticle	
Collect of the Day	
Prayers	
Lord's Prayer	
Benedicamus	Intonation pitches
Offering	
Hymn	
Sermon	
Prayer	
Benediction	Pitch given

Appendix D
Using Handbells in the Service of Evening Prayer

Portion of Service	Handbell Use
Service of Light	Pitch given
Psalmody	
Prayer	
Second Psalm (opt. *LW*)	Psalm Tone Accompaniment
Psalm Prayer (*LBW*)	
Hymn	
Reading(s)	
Gospel Canticle	
Litany	Pitch given
Lord's Prayer	
Benedicamus	Pitch given
Offering	
Hymn	
Sermon	
Prayer	
Benediction	Pitch given

Appendix E
Suggestions for Further Reading

Bedford, P. *An Introduction to English Handbell Tune Reading.* Chelmsford, 1974.
Parry, S. B. *The Story of Handbells.* Boston, 1957.
Proulx, R. *Tintinnabulum: The Liturgical Use of Handbells.* Chicago, 1980.
Tufts, N. P. *The Art of Handbell Ringing.* New York, 1973.

Appendix F
Handbell Organization and Principal Manufacturers of Handbells

Handbell Organization

The American Guild of English Handbell Ringers, Inc.
601 West Riverview Drive
Dayton, Ohio 45406

Principal Manufacturers of Handbells

I. T. Verdin Company
2021 Eastern Avenue
Cincinnati, Ohio 45202

Malmark, Inc.
21 Bell Lane
New Britain, Pennsylvania 18901

Petit & Fritsen Bell Foundry
Bellfounderstreet, Aarle-Rixel, Holland
U.S.A. Agent: G.I.A.
7404 S. Mason Avenue
Chicago, Illinois 60638

Schulmerich Carillons, Inc.
Carillon Hill
Sellersville, Pennsylvania 18960

Whitechapel Bell Foundry
32 & 34 Whitechapel Road
London E1 1DY, England

Notes

1. Additional information on the use of bells in the ancient world, as well as in more recent times, may be found in Price, Percival, "Handbell," *The New Grove Dictionary of Music and Musicians*. For the use of bells in medieval times and in the Renaissance, see P. H. Lang, *Music in Western Civilization* (New York: Norton, 1941), p. 80 ff; and G. Reese, *Music in the Middle Ages* (New York: Norton, 1940), *passim*.
2. *Luther's Works,* American Edition, 54, p. 164. Hereafter LW.
3. LW 40, pp. 311-12.
4. Ibid., p. 312.

Acknowledgments

From *Lutheran Worship,* copyright © 1982 Concordia Publishing House: Psalm tones. Used by permission.
From *Lutheran Book of Worship,* copyright © 1978. Concordia Publishing House representing the publishers and copyright holders. Used by permission. From *The Holy Communion,* Setting One: Music of "Holy, holy, holy Lord"; music and text of "Thank the Lord and sing his praise." Also the psalm tones.
International Consultation on English Texts: The canticle text "Holy, holy, holy Lord."
Gelobt sei Gott: Harmonization by Carl Schalk, copyright © GIA Publications. Used by permission.
Earth and All Stars: Tune by David N. Johnson, copyright © 1968 Augsburg Publishing House. Used by permission.